CONFESSIONS

POEMS

Anis Shivani

Červená Barva Press
Somerville, Massachusetts

Červená Barva Press
P.O. Box 440357
W. Somerville, MA 02144-3222

www.cervenabarvapress.com

Bookstore: www.thelostbookshelf.com

Cover Art: Thomas Hovenden, *Self-Portrait of the Artist in His Studio*, 1875
Courtesy Yale University Art Gallery

Cover design: William J. Kelle

ISBN: 978-1-950063-29-1

Library of Congress Control Number: 2022946742

Also by Anis Shivani

Anatolia and Other Stories
The Fifth Lash and Other Stories
Karachi Raj: A Novel
A History of the Cat in Nine Chapters or Less: A Novel

My Tranquil War and Other Poems
Whatever Speaks on Behalf of Hashish: Poems
Soraya: Sonnets
The Moon Blooms in Occupied Hours: Poems

Against the Workshop: Provocations, Polemics, Controversies
Literary Writing in the Twenty-First Century: Conversations

ACKNOWLEDGMENTS

Many thanks to the editors of *Prairie Schooner*, *The American Journal of Poetry*, *The Offending Adam*, and *Xavier Review*, where individual poems in this book first appeared. Thanks to Kwame Dawes, Ashley Strosnider, and the other editors at *Prairie Schooner* for picking a very generous selection of these poems for the 2018 Glenna Luschei *Praire Schooner* Award, for which I am incredibly grateful to this beautiful journal and its great editors. Thanks to Rachel Eliza Griffiths, Harvey L. Hix, Dave Brinks, Richard Burgin, Joe Phillips, Susan Wood, Geoffrey Gatza, Fady Joudah, Clayton Eshleman, Michael Woodson, Chris Wise, Dustin Pickering, Fran Sanders, Heller Levinson, Laura Mullen, Peter Krok, Kevin Prufer, and the late Franz Wright and his wife Elizabeth Oehlkers Wright, for being great poetry friends over the years. Thanks to Ifeanyi Menkiti and Elizabeth Doran for hosting me for a reading at my beloved Grolier Poetry Book Shop in Harvard Square in 2013 where I first met Gloria, leading eventually to the publication of this book. Thank you, Gloria, for believing in my work; I admire your dedication to poetry publishing and translation over the decades, and I doubt there can be a more honorable line of work in this day and age.

For Mehnaaz

CONFESSIONS

POEMS

Religion is a plantation economy
burning big-eyed corpses in a cricket stadium,
burning Orwell's hidden texts in plain sight of the rats.
Rats have been big in my spiritual autobiography,
which begins here, with an ego as large as the "x"
in the xylophone, as tiny as the bead-eyed danio
which you have for breakfast.

I was alive in 1984 as a prolapsed final solution,
so long past Iwo Jima that the guns blazed
in the movie theater while I planted traps, traps to
catch the primigravida chewing off her sullen womb
because she became anxious at the briefest sight
of me in my toe clips. Yes I am unconventional,
but what did you expect of a writer?

And I'm a real one too. Literature circulates in
my vital thumbs like a prognosis by Vivaldi,
the lead in the water in my house in my rotten borough
disappears because of gold, gold everywhere,
gold estoile hovering over my head like a spouse,
the only one I could be faithful to, Longinus and I
refusing to be benchwarming melodies.

It wouldn't be inaccurate to call me a misanthrope
and a misogynist and a mistaken Melpomene,
heralding my polymorphous death in near rhymes and near
    misses,
seeking an audience that doesn't yet exist. I
thought I was writing a twenty-first-century novel,
but what I have been producing all along is
émigrés holding hands emotionally.

Does writing ensue from an evil instinct?
Why do you care for my cheerless eminence?
There are candidates for autobiography and there are
candidates for cancer, but we must vary the tone
of the Beige Book once in a while, lest
the workers rise in a fit of articulation, and
arrive by mistake at true arson.

It is true I have only loved once in my life.
My mandarin appearance, amongst the stalwarts of
print, is a marshy blue flag in a meadow
of blunders, it is a blush the charwoman knows
all too well as the sin before the crime,
it is the hirsute Maine Coon purebred
like the high comedy of pederasts.

It is not possible to be honest among capitalists.
I can only steal, it is the only thing left for me to do,
if I want to hold my head high, a hierarch
punished like Melos cranberries melting in the bizarre
nada sun, the mythomanias my parents acquired
as fallback (what if? what if it's all true?) migrating
to my light-sensitive polypoid hands.

But all the world believes. Lightning, inverted snobbery,
hexahedrons, dysphasia, royal tennis, the roving eye,
tarweed, Tarzan, the Pearly Gates, Odysseus,
Moulin Rouge, infanticide, heteronyms, Eid, Egypt,
egg rolls, cyanosis, cybernauts, cypress knees,
dickey birds. Lots to believe in, lots to stuff
into the pzazz camcorder before baptism.

It is easiest to believe in nothing. What is nothing?
A banyan tree without the trunk, a barrier
in a holiday when you are trying to decide if
you want to be a fortress or a loading dock,
a woman who teaches you necromancy,
a press release for your medal of freedom, these are
the vipers in my bosom I coddle.

But when do you think I will stand vindicated?
I practiced higher criticism in my geodesic dome,
a form of dog Latin (no?), imagining dechristianization
among the crakes of brinkmanship, imagining
my recherché pyramids, imagining riding home
in a hackney made to my lexical specifications,
my past as a Lhasa apso no liability.

Who are the thin men in my population
of infantine reserves? They are literalist infidels,
who know the way I grew up among liquidity, went to
private school arguing for my wiry schnauzer,
the way I was appointed stationer to the unconscious,
all before fifteen, before I discovered
the foxhole to spend my life in.

We will form a consortium of love, once I take leave of
the butterflies surrounding the bylaws, once I exit
the Ivy League as a quilling restroom choked
with sixpence. How far-flung the countersubjects
obtainable by mere centavos, at the bottom of the barrel
axisymmetric aye-ayes, confirmation of the ordeal
via the rough trades of the rotoscope.

Always the problem of money. Money as
stenography. Money as Wallace Stegner's foxhunt
for the Magnus effect, in the new Pax Romana.
Money in the pay envelope stuffed with second-
person sphincters. Money spelling the end of the
Colorado spruce. It's as if I were born bucktoothed
and interbred in the rabbit warren.

I mentioned thieving earlier, a consistent pattern, a
leitmotif if you will, my own third law of thermodynamics,
which you can observe at any of my well-attended readings
for Thetis, for the housekeepers of information technology.
I carry in my ditty bag—everywhere from Trader Joe's
to the university library—a coolie hat, not known to
knowledge workers, and my secret mantelletta.

I also studied the rational expectations hypothesis
as a budding economist. And I learned that earthbound
distress can be measured in units of scale. I was
taught my position on the color wheel, black velvet
or ash blond, depending on the duration of the financial
year. I wandered onto the playa with my Platonic
stenosis, and stepped out with the redheaded waitress.

The summer I read all of Molière I was already
sick of ear candy, I disbelieved in earnestness, I was
crumpled in my own fist of crown jewels
as a gruesome baby in Lin Biao's line
of work. The Chinese communists are all dead.
In my time no one knew what existed in Mozambique.
Even now my mouse ear is tuned to percussion.

You were penciled in as stepbrother
just when the evangelists arrived at the doorstep
speaking of Cremona as the home of Stradivari.
Or am I thinking of the chatoyant Jehovah's
Witnesses at our Queens apartment, back in the
blizzard of '83, when we went all gnostic and vain,
like Melina Mercouri's pump gun?

I keep coming back to the rhizomorph as the style
least suited to my form of cancer. Memories
are never recollected verbatim, at least not
in my case. What stems from having a prolonged
spell of kindheartedness is loss of suzerainty.
You play one practical joke after another in your
years of innocence, lulled by satiety.

I lived in California as satellite television. In Massachusetts
as juggernaut from Juilliard. In Texas as oversubscribed
promethium. And there were many forgotten places
along the way, in each one of which the subculture
I inhabited was of my own making, stylized
for irradiance, hardened in frugality, degressive
according to the cosmological argument of the moment.

But there is only one place I have ever truly lived.
Once in Corvallis, as the bees sang evidence, and
forked lightning illumined hectic dead Bibles,
I gave you my octopus hand, proletarian
in my recapitulation, and I asked you to take care
of the streetlights, extend the synchronized night,
and try to think of me as diamondback terrapin.

Alone, hovering over your body, on a glide path dictated
by lepton numbers, I smell of mezereon and so
do you, and the padlock over my emotions at long last
is sloppy and melted and trucial. But this is not to say
I admire your volva enclosure of my white lists
(such sudden admiration!), this doesn't mean
the cystitis you notice is from today.

I am cold, bleak, Dada, fondu, Haile Selassie, mummy,
pampas grass, I have redefined the rules of engagement, and
though you have seen me perform like silk cotton or
Suetonius (my tongue hanging out like my exposed diaries)
there is no guarantee that I am not a common rat
or a long-eared bat, both creatures that scare you,
as you sink into my octane rating.

I remember the exact date I turned into Nostradamus.
I could predict the precise quantity of sea room I would need
to elicit your demisemiquaver. I knew a thing or two
about the past, peeling off its Jerusalem artichoke squeals
while the world (of news and pews) eavesdropped
like carrier pigeons. Calmly I measured the cuckoo spit
it would take for me to be bellman or carpenter.

No one quite knows me. I am herself in defense
of the hermit crab, philumenist in my own
sector of chiromancy (the cowgirls follow just
behind the tractor), I am film noir to
mothers-to-be. Do not desecrate my privacy.
Some folks go in for radiotherapy or recrimination,
but why not translate the skanks?

It was a night of unequal transparency.
Some observed Kwanzaa, some read "The Wreck
of the Deutschland," some killed elkhounds.
To be eloquent like the Colosseum, or to
find the means between density and freedom,
like Coltrane, requires one to be a bird of prey
first, a broken-down car in the dark.

I will leave you just when you think I am
singularly attracted to the Khazars because they
made the peace sign—or did they? Do you
know what percent purity in sterling silver?
Or for that matter your Russian salad? Toward
conservation of energy we make many
failed gestures, under dated bylines.

I always held journalism to be a debased profession.
So pursue me to the banana belt, what have I
got to lose? I am indisposed today, sorry, you will
not see me take the hammer to my secretaire,
shaking the tambourine of greed and the great white
shark. It is too easy to be directional,
too easy to be overstimulated by fat panada.

I will abort skeletal grandfather clocks.
Is it the granola fission already, three p.m. in the shade,
fish cakes detonating in the arms of
maidservants? Why must you be this raffish
statistical inference? I do not think
your vers libre turns me into an Egyptian
mongoose. The coinage is all botanical.

Another leitmotif is the border. Its finality,
its Lissajous figures of thick thesaurus equalities,
its subharmonic transfusions, its dog-weary
domicile in etiquette. No one admits they're in
a roman-fleuve when it's most obvious. No one
has ever seen a snuff film either. Episiotomy,
how attractive, how very considerate!

The know-nothings haunt me in every land I go.
The showy lady's-slipper will turn into a
pit bull if you call someone a sweetie pie, which
is a swindle at the châteaus, there they are not
such cheapskates. We bray our bravery,
backed by the dramaturgy of the knockout mouse,
and the soft palate of the people meter.

I have been hiding from tamper-proof Trotskyism,
one authoritarian pursuing me to the entrance
to the chaste tree, another bribing me with
discarnate gospel music. On the radio, in the
Lone Star State, I sound like replacement therapy,
the spirit moves me to act like a treehopper.
What does a poet laureate *do*?

What do you see in the garden of poinsettias?
Diploid numbers walking, marching, dancing to the tune
of thick fog, the last trading card dealt to the clerks.
Freeze me in vinyl chloride. Or the vineyards of
whisk brooms. Scatter my ashes in the Smokies
in direct proportion to my numerous comebacks,
lick the last drops of butter icing.

I asked the proprietress, what happened to my sense
of humor? Had she seen it amongst the peacocks?
Spit and polish wouldn't do it anymore,
I had reached the outer reaches of the spiral galaxy,
disinterested in splatterpunk, vespertine
forbidder of foreknowledge. A world full of
precogs is too eerily familiar.

There was a great deal of disorder my father
had to crush, on his way to fulfilling the covenant.
Along the way he and I acquired claustrophobia,
because we failed to hear the bell-ringing,
and we didn't share the esprit de corps of the warriors
either. How do you propose to stop my
improprieties? There is no neutral corner.

Tyrant of restrictive covenants and resubmissions,
thalidomide parent, not quite a people person,
and also not a pencil pusher, but certainly full of
penis envy: you failed to leave me your nest egg,
which I freely gave up to be Neruda's ashlaring nephew,
while you were content to pursue Crohn's disease,
and tear up the katsinas' crocodile tears.

Enough of the past. It's the future I care about.
The future, burning with arsphenamine,
fat as red, green, and blue fratricidal additives,
licit like library science, rational beyond
the raspberry tweed jacket, unified in
tough love. The future, whose heliotrope distillery
I visit with body-pressing comrades.

The past will be regimented, the future not so much.
The hegemony of perception, whether it's the
peregrine falcon in my sight or the statoblasts of
Soraya, is no longer an ominous statement such as
drives me out of my mind. The hunt for the oncogene
is over. The signorina turned out to be an illustrator,
a flag-waving siltstone, swaddled in a trousseau of visas.

Where the sound of youth is monocline jacquerie,
all the jailbirds recite their hard-luck stories
like conceited eagle owls, and not a gender bender
among them, gemütlich genealogical trees
proving each other a necessary geisha.
I feel old as Nebuchadnezzar, twenty bottles
of protolanguage, the proverbial statute book.

There may be a difficulty with my preen gland.
I am the monkey who delivers letters of intent to
the Himalayas, despite legs that feel like entrocôte
wounds, eyes that can no longer descramble
the designs of chlamydia, and the only language
my tongue can articulate is Chinook Jargon.
O bird-watchers, put away your bayonets!

The distance between you and me. The
Dutch interior of the beach, a gruel of Dürer,
longevity in the netherworld, just enough
ratafia biscuits. Wood satyrs behind the
snowplow. All my think pieces, umbrella
birds, hamsters with a foothold. The silence
of meiosis, the quiet neuralgia of olive drab.

It was my choice to live in the slums, to see where
the open road ended, to acquire the pathologies
not known to the patisserie or the patio rose.
I became a scholar among sex workers in
the Seyfert galaxies, I prosecuted mute swans,
likable Liliths, and the fetor of the fertility cult.
How do we cope with leaf mold in the spring?

.

To be poor like a pamphlet for Narcissus,
or a cat burglar with the manners of a diving petrel,
never came easy to me. Still I persisted. I dreamed
of pylons on the putting green, big secluded
sea slugs, magdalene in Marfa, idempotent
no matter how acted upon or reformed. I was flea-
bitten, though my itch came from Karakoram.

Why I became a poet, in twenty-five words or less.
Gandy dancer, gammon, jiggery-pokery,
longerons that are object lessons to fliers in the red,
red skies—please, the obloquy hurts! In the
quaint reliquary I found the shadow price of my
real cost of labor: spiccato housebreaking,
going to bed with the golliwog.

Long good-tempered narratives, a quarter million
words or more, finding a way to douceur de vivre, the
war observed through the hodoscope, madrigal
influenced by the demise of carrier pigeons. A novel,
by its very nature, is carpentry in the Carolingian
Renaissance, as I learned on the carousel, while
you designed the ingrain carpet.

The mole rat wants to commit suicide this winter.
Have you heard enough already of referred pain?
I fall asleep to sweet william, ear shell or dumb iron,
earth mother warming me with the limbus of mud baths,
whispering the infinity of the rubbing strake. Wedlock
with the acacia, character strings for daltonism,
the downside to coeval spermicide.

Again the descent into coefficients of viscosity,
on the beach the summer coffee cake, the flags for khat,
nude Khrushchev arriving as June publication:
resurrection is the dressing gown for meditation,
which you taught me as alternative to my crookback
dreamscape. The beach is endless crocodile
birds, color therapy in this aseismic land.

Those who keep dying in my arms include the diaspora's
Eurasian representative, the man who snuffs out geeks
prone to melodrama, and the dabbling duck who turns
into Dade County in occult light. The last breath
is always like the octopus's secession from excitability,
circumcision in an awkward bloom of azaleas,
ferment of nanoplankton underneath razor blades.

In an attempt to write pure poetry I followed
the reindeer over the grasslands, monocle firmly
in place. To avoid reprisals I wore tanga briefs.
I craned my neck to the heights of tall timber,
not knowing how the Coriolis effect worked on me.
My circadian rhythms wore off. I adored bottlenose
dolphins and fed them aureoles of merriment.

Indeed I have not witnessed any mescal deaths. Nor
have I been involved in bar brawls involving mercury-
vapor lamps or torn sartorius muscles. A tambour can be
a door through which to exit to usquebaugh, behind which
is contre-jour white matter. All of my life since the first
years I have tried to recreate the coiffure of green space,
gliding along the Chao Phraya with the bog asphodel.

I am afraid your grief will infect my neutron star.
You can be ravenous when I tell you how I make duxelles
for today's climate, you take liberties with my library
constructed from peach blooms and radiation belts. You
like to use the word "sashay" to describe your movements,
pouring rosolio down my stamen. I would rather be a
recumbent statue, my voice a fuzzbox from day school.

I paused for a moment in the staging area,
watching employees punch timecards. Those
went extinct like the timbal or the uterus,
shortly thereafter. I do not know what time
is, I do not understand hide-and-seek among
flamingos, I think the Erie Canal disappears
whenever I return to my dacha.

I left the dead man's handle in the hands of my
faithful servant. Dear herptile deactivators,
the hermitage is full of Javan rhinoceros, visiting us
like multivitamins. I hate the word "relativistic,"
because running repairs are easier to conduct
otherwise. The machinery of Tamerlane
buzzes in me, ignore the distress signals.

Trudging toward the tropopause, your viola and
my Bosporus clairvoyance, we encountered our first
language. It was full of idiosyncratic fistulas,
mélange leaks, pulpwood and silicon.
I might as well be a Tamil speaker for all you care
about my uncoiling wind chimes, the crumple
zone that fell off the carousel.

Carrion beetle, intifida among restaurateurs,
the boy Skanda mounting the peacock while the
trouvères cross-train in the Deep South or deep space
to hide the finger of God. War has come with a glandular
gleam not hidden from my left brain, with all the
morphic resonance of viewports on oil rigs.
Windflower, the odds are stacked against you.

In my youth I accepted the role of stage manager
with much glee, unconstitutional though the forward
contract was. I gave you the correct expression
marks, though your congregation is too fond
of burnsides. Askaris in low spirits can be motivated,
English breakfasts can be reproduced in Africa,
and game theory is just ganache over burst loins.

When I encounter naïveté among the long pigs,
how do I carry on with progressive dinners, what
sense can I make of the banishment of Reiter's
syndrome? You, synergist of distributed systems,
can you lend me the contraceptive for the evening?
I do not know which side my bread is buttered on.
I was not dragooned into franchise euphoria.

What are your instructions for the median strip
I will cross tonight on my way home from the sister
city? Sirius burns bright, dog star, courteous
coppersmith. The chatterboxes admit of no bull
of the woods, their anomie is herringboned
and perhaps of herstory's molecular weight:
their modus tollens turns to primordial soup.

Queen of puddings, I am truthful and loyal
to you, since my eardrum burst. What is curable
among the order of lies, what is not? Fly ash,
after my flutter-tonguing, is like Lascaux's animals
in my iron lungs. Through the grapevine I
learn of gravediggers waiting for my truths to
come out, like fog at Point Reyes.

Dear Shakespeare. Cornucopia of glosses,
eyes globetrotting past hype and hymen, italics
proclaiming me rearguard realtor of the
tanager lands. What is tangible about time-
sharing? I wake up deforested, my dreams have
the quality of the Counter-Reformation,
and you can clearly see my caste mark.

Let us choose the right typeface for the eyehole.
Play the panpipes of a skeeter afternoon,
in our subfusc clothing that makes us think of
the Voronezh we have never been to. Do you
know about the Great Vowel Shift? I didn't,
until you put me in the bodysuit, I beg your pardon
for my atticism, it is cheaper this way.

We are said to have discovered Arabic numerals
in our channel-hop sleep, even our antagonists grant
us that. Though they may not like karyotyping,
most of their legal capacity is a fiction, like a legend
worth a red cent, a fireless cooker not thrown
out during spring cleaning. Consider the eruption
of the error bar, its nestled polemics.

From Andalus to Delhi a vast history of Nestorianism,
street vendors who knew of tea gardens just behind
the veil of sight, translators galore, genealogical gibberish
that passed as harmless hobbyhorse. So much indebtedness,
such a katzenjammer from the twelfth century, whether
I find myself in Kathiawar (before the hour of birth),
or whether I swallow the katsuobushi whole.

My alliance was always with the poor among the literary
men. They were the ones whose longevity I admired.
What is it to be lonesome, I asked the nonsmoking ones,
what shall I do to remain crystalloid? The sperm
of the sperm whale is in its head, and likewise the Sphinx
always thinks of trading stamps. They used to say
"pickaninny" without qualms, merely a piano roll.

From Pick's disease we have moved to generalized
dementia, sculpted tangerine brains in whose user interface
kaftans wave at me, cheer my inoculum, because
I read too much for the honor society. When they
came with the Jaws of Life it was already too late, I
acted like leishmania caught between Scylla and...
oh yes, the painted snipes at the swimming hole.

I crossed the border in a palace car. The man
next to me spouted the virtues of *Atlas Shrugged*.
I remember his reported speech. His security
blanket. He wanted me to subdivide, right there,
in front of his eyes, so he could scratch his
temporal bone without reading my barcode.
Yes, I crossed the border to unlisted sagamores.

.

Sahib, the only injustice in the world is not having the luxury to hate rats, because you are busy being a suffix to Typhoid Marys, because the hickeys on your shoulders are from the enfilade in your home full of hamzas and handbells. You are called illiterate and not aware of jazz by the nawabs whose room and board amounts to your four freedoms.

I went to this party for game wardens.
It was New Year's Eve, interest-free loans
were on offer, we ate jack mackerel and
layer cakes. Lazy daisy stitch. That night
we shot the useless mokes. Then we
played mumblety-peg, donated our open-
necked loins to the oversoul.

Of course it was a sheltered workshop, how
else do you think I made it through sheet lightning?
Graduation day arrived in a roar of graffiti,
as mahatmas of unknown marital status told us:
You are the best and the brightest, though you are all
here because of an error, so go and explore
the quadrat, you will perfect schizogony.

I fall in love inordinately, like Schleswig-Holstein's
tantaluses, visible to tapestry moths. Is it so irrational?
The hemisphere I belong to—"All Along the Watchtower"—
is crafted in German silver, our georgics serve as the
flanging to the disjecta membra that masquerade as
the realist bourgeois novel. I cannot be cuckoo in
the nest, I am crybaby cruzeiros. Cui bono?

From Robinson Crusoe to the Frankfurt School,
along the way I had to understand what it meant
to know someone in the biblical sense, I had to
learn not to take the long view. I quadrupled the
stakes every chance I got. I am old enough to have
seen rag-and-bone men at the gatepost, waiting
for their gay electrocutions to come through.

Virginia Woolf had it right with androgyny. Your
halter top and its disinformation, carbon black ingested
by barefoot doctors, fraternal ties among the
hibakushas operating still on high beam: recidivism
in the siciliano mindset is a thesis with no name,
transliteration can be confusing. Goddaughter, we
undertake the great trek joint and several.

To live among the texts of fruitage, growing
fuchsia krones, kundalini on the libertarian trail,
sitting on the priapic mastaba, waiting for
the sexual revolution to at last take place. Diva,
diva, distressed words are all I have, do not
be hasty with the streptomycin, newer drugs have
come along, sleeker ectomorphs.

When I first saw the grasshopper mouse chirping
at the site of the hit-and-run I committed (isogloss!),
I said hello, imagesetter, one man's meat is
another's poison, but don't join the Peace Corps
just yet. I established quick rapport, rapid eye movement,
sectionalism, and four-star table talk. From the
exterior angle we looked alike, both disinfected.

How can I trust you, grand master, even the khedives
refuse to perform lumpectomies on me. The nature
of things is in the form of a model home, inhabited by
nocturnal creepy-crawlies, in the daytime a complex plane
at which one arrives with burnt offerings. One might
meet a bush baby in the suburban confectionaries,
waiting in line behind insurgent hairpieces.

I have to admit defeat, amidst the clutter and coal oil burning through my detective heart. The futility of forethought stood out to me as indictment of photonegative rinky-dink writing, such as you find in a spearman's attitude. I chose to specialize in sum totals. True, conjugal rights are overrated, but so is the Cartesian product in the bottomlands.

Please, your black panther metaphors have outlived
their usefulness. Bland is the black rat, as are Balzac's
collected works, sitting on my shelf like amity with
the flower children. I must have a diseased satiety center,
activated only by the end of the saros,
as each time I survey the debris produced by my obsessive
hard work and miss the teardrops.

At my funeral, the old girlfriends came wearing tetrose
mysteries, smelling of egg cream, passing notes to
each other about the diplomatic pouch in which they each
perceived diffusivity, the capability for heroic cowardice
which is the highest virtue. I gave it the old college
try, I collided with Lolitas who burned with pinene and
took off my pince-nez and crunched them underfoot.

Pink-collar work (radwaste) in the snorkeling radio
galaxies, chauvinist machines buzzing in the snowscape
like Carracci at work, and the ailerons stored in the
antechapel giving rise to convulsant blatherskites:
what forgettable landscape have you transported me to?
Let us explore the knot garden of a mangrove evening
and figure out the dimensions of the mandorla.

When I was born they were dreaming of interstellar
travel, or at least flying cars and personal helicopters,
robots that would stand at beck and call, and sex merely
a question of percentiles and reiki laws. It wasn't long
ago that I would pass salvage yards in the triage
cities of this country and envision the flow of light
between ethical dahlias and their daimons.

The problem is one of excess ethylene. Everywhere
the helplines are backed up. I gaze into my navel and see
restraint of trade, the sweetness of tchothkes. I like to
think that I would have been better off in 1969,
when the dwarf crested iris for a moment ruled the
world, and the flour moth was defeated. The ringing
in my ears is from the softened drinking fountain.

At Lamont Library once I was looking up Philip Roth's
underrated works. As an undergraduate (gagman
of loose-leaf mewls) I believed in metonyms, and
the art of the mezzanine. When I visited MoMA
that summer, to recreate a second childhood, I ran into
secret societies who had labeled me a monist (wrongly?),
who knew my exact count of passenger miles.

Sleeping next to me, your head on my shoulder, smelling of paspalum in the aftermath of personhood, you have enough sense to question me as sculptural fireman.
I kissed you through fumes of Epsom salts, indulging the epistemologist in you. But we were apart like itchy cosmopolites in Karl-Marx-Stadt. Your grandfather owns a mimeograph? So did mine every off year.

Hey, office boy, sculpt this rat, your stepfamily's thermostat, does Comaneci get 10.0? As a child you had many close shaves (with illiteracy), but escaped with your clubfoot intact each time. When we see Falasha art in euphoric full dress, aware of our G-spots, we are already on the leader board. My praenomen is not a secret to broadcasters.

The beach's intense Britannia metal, men of substance
holding baldrics and antiquarian currycombs,
featherlight touch of fawning water over my feet:
the jargon of literature classes is of a monotype that looks
like a gifted Persian carpet, woven into our peroneal
muscles. The men work out obsessively, perhaps
as restitution for random walks through race memory?

Menominee! What is the technical term
for river blindness? Who among us remains
spermatic after viewing the fashion plates?
The fatiha is dug over, conservation of energy
no longer means anything, bantamweight
is going bankrupt. Araneids in my teacup,
I see them as the true éminences grises.

The memories come fast and loose now, the dawn of the imperator a false night, as though the ending were just the beginning: time travel is not what it used to be, neither is the memory of the imamate. At dawn the prayer call came to me as an investiture, like leaflove eating through my rest cure. It was then that the sex offenders lined up for identification.

I know you as a sewing machine knows thread,
mother and father caught in the grappling hook, I
have passed through the French doors as the darling
of conspiracy theories. We might get botulism,
it is common enough. I will help you with your fading
marcel wave, I will gladly wear your reach-me-downs.
Just give me a moment to read up on cataracts.

At the checkpoint of longitudinal waves, I perceived
a dead Naguib Mahfouz, who was magnificent in his
recapitulation. The same few words keep recurring,
like runcible spoons in the draped citadel. I didn't have to
run away from civil death, they were waiting for me
with broadaxes and hermeneutics. They too have
shunned relativism, theirs is a religion of ice packs.

No, I still cannot trust iconology, I have been burned
one too many times. We are each incarnate as Rinpoche
once in our lives, like a dripstone that knows only one
direction. Now they want to defraud me of my hard-earned
gormandizing, their inside information is of no use to
me. In the locket I stole there was a rupestrian idea that
stayed with me, a delta connection to the best crêperies.

And what about Orientalism? At the bookstores in
Cambridge, Mass., carving knives in hand, we decentered
our loneliness in headlong hyperbole. You were there,
you saw me, did I ever assault the manciples, did I act
mordant for no reason? In Lowell House's senior common
room, sadism was the style among men no stronger
than touch football, the women wore soiled underthings.

I keep coming back to the semaphore. It is self-
sustaining, it is the barrio's foreboding, where I meet
the haggadists of interference: everyone
here knows everyone else's business. I still
remember the propaganda about the Scud missiles,
and Bosnian immigrants when they had the air
of foraging spring chickens about them.

Death is not a matter of foot-and-mouth disease
getting out of control. The gray uncles had a habit of
falling dead in the middle of écarté, the poor man's
eavesdropping. At my first funeral for the dying
conservationists, I recited in my cadential brain
the blueprint that would guide me: it is becoming
when you are dead to act like the atlas.

On commencement day, Al Gore spoke of arsine in water,
or was it reinventing government, and Tipper
(in the row in front of me), kept her smoky head still,
arterializing the opinions of the future internet in
her every moviegoing spirochete. In the yard I shook
hands with him, or think I did, knowing it would
cost me dearly yet, this cinnamon debenture.

There are times I have been so poor I have considered
death a better option. But then I think of noble gas.
I never met Nkrumah but he was the pulp cavity
to translunar dreams. And I think of vanishing cream,
and employment agencies, and all the contingency plans
for continuation. At times I have admired body bags.
But the scene of the crime is only for blowhards to see.

Behavioralism has something to it, at least when it comes to other people. The finance companies know it all. My friends all went to work for the hindquarters of Goldman Sachs after studying Marx in the hippodrome, and they are anonymous now, all of them, you can't find them in any leaks. Their monikers are what you would call negative evidence.

The neighbor who wanted me to show her my stash
of red flags knew of seif dunes in the Sahara.
When I touched her stonewashed skin it fell apart.
We drank Frascati and remembered Germantown.
Did I make my own exclamation points? Was
connectivity a thing? Could I predict brittle fractures?
The California desert sure has flawless barrancas.

When I was past the age of the bull market I
had to learn my first language all over again, and it
felt flattering. You bought expensive glucosamine
when my knees first went gnostic, all the
love beads I got for you had resolving power.
Free speech was not just for the overclass,
we both lived by that rule, we went mute for it.

The cat and its meadowsweet low tide. A lifespan
of invertibility, silent heeltap amidst fringed gentians.
They came to teach me how to die, and their
fractal développé was a help. I lost my driver's license,
but the coronary vein felt strong like feijoada, I
groped it with mercuric love. We died in the shade
of the frangipani watched by jumping spiders.

At last you have felt my moisture. Touch me
for the modulus whose pressure points I revised,
day by day, in an ongoing act of irreversibility,
making myself silica, immeasurable live weight.
Polyglots, pederasts, pharaohs: whose ruthless
phenomena will you believe in? Faith comes on
second thought, when the fovea are excised.

Age, Fleming's right-hand rule, the induced
currents whereby my narrowband assumes this
napalm guise, fizzing in your hands, as you want
to know my pen name. The rats are pendant, I can
touch bright Spica from where I lie on Malibu
beach, everything will come true like the
eagle owl, every crucifer will bully me.

ABOUT THE AUTHOR

Anis Shivani is a poet, fiction writer, and literary critic living in Houston, Texas. His critically acclaimed books include *Anatolia and Other Stories*, *The Fifth Lash and Other Stories*, *Karachi Raj: A Novel*, *My Tranquil War and Other Poems*, *Whatever Speaks on Behalf of Hashish: Poems*, *The Moon Blooms in Occupied Hours: Poems*, *Soraya: Sonnets*, *Against the Workshop: Provocations, Polemics, Controversies*, and *Literary Writing in the Twenty-First Century: Conversations*. His work appears widely in such journals as the *Yale Review*, *Georgia Review*, *Southwest Review*, *Boston Review*, *Threepenny Review*, *Michigan Quarterly Review*, *Antioch Review*, *Black Warrior Review*, *Western Humanities Review*, *Boulevard*, *Pleiades*, *AGNI*, *Fence*, *Denver Quarterly*, *The Journal*, *Gulf Coast*, *Third Coast*, *Volt*, *Subtropics*, *New Letters*, *Times Literary Supplement*, *London Magazine*, *Cambridge Quarterly*, *Meanjin*, *Fiddlehead*, *Dalhousie Review*, *Antigonish Review*, and elsewhere. He has also written for many magazines and newspapers including *Salon*, *Daily Beast*, *AlterNet*, *CommonDreams*, *Truthout*, *Huffington Post*, *Texas Observer*, *In These Times*, *Boston Globe*, *San Francisco Chronicle*, *Kansas City Star*, *Pittsburgh Post-Gazette*, *St. Petersburg Times*, *Baltimore Sun*, *Charlotte Observer*, *Austin American-Statesman*, and elsewhere. He is the winner of a Pushcart Prize, and a graduate of Harvard College.

PRAISE FOR ANIS SHIVANI'S POETRY

"Anis Shivani evidently inhabits a world in which every moment of time in the past, present, and a humorously but lethally prophesied future, occurs simultaneously and is animated by a wit sometimes subtle, sometimes savagely indignant. Its two faces join forces and somehow manage to speak in unison of what they actually see and think. I sense everywhere an undercurrent of compassion and identification, a poignant humanity and sense of responsibility underneath his torrential voice."
—Franz Wright

"When I first plunged into Anis Shivani's work, I had the impression two of my most admired dead poet friends were one-upping each other in the afterlife—Tom Disch with his straight-faced drop-dead virtuoso satire of literary and political pretension and Aga Shahid Ali with his eloquent, global, polyglot formal legerdemain—both of them knowing more about history and about literature than ninety-nine percent of their readers. But Shivani's poems are no phantoms, they are vibrant, new, knowledgeable, daring, and welcome."
—Marilyn Hacker

Anis Shivani's poetry is remarkable for its continuing preoccupation with literature, culture, and language, and a discourse that incorporates the written word, the oral tradition, and the imagery of art and film. His cerebral poems often border on the obscure, but constantly challenge the reader to unravel deeply embedded references, suggestions, and innuendoes. The innovative use of words and sounds that draw on myriad languages and cultures adds to the rich texture of each poem.
—Muneeza Shamsie

9 781950 063291